Method in Metaphysics

The Aquinas Lecture, 1950

Method
in
Metaphysics

Under the Auspices of the Aristotelian Society
of Marquette University

BY

ROBERT J. HENLE, S.J.
A.B., A.M., Ph.L., S.T.L.

MARQUETTE UNIVERSITY PRESS
MILWAUKEE
1951

110
H38m

Nihil Obstat

        Francis Wade, S.J., censor deputatus
        Milwaukiae, die 8 mensis Januarii, 1951

Imprimatur

        ✠ Moyses E. Kiley
        Archiepiscopus Milwaukiensis
        Milwaukiae, die 12 mensis Januarii, 1951

Imprimi Potest

        Daniel H. Conway, S.J.
        Praepositus Provincialis
        Provinciae Missourianae
        die 25 mensis Novembris, 1950

Prefatory

The Aristotelian Society of Marquette University each year invites a scholar to deliver a lecture in honor of St. Thomas Aquinas. Customarily delivered on the Sunday nearest March 7, the feast-day of the Society's patron saint, these lectures are called the Aquinas lectures.

In 1950 the Society had the pleasure of recording the lecture of the Reverend Robert J. Henle, S.J.

Father Henle was born Sept. 12, 1909 at Muscatine, Iowa. He received the A.B. degree in 1931; A.M. in 1932; the Licentiate in Philosophy in 1935, all from St. Louis University; the Licentiate in Sacred Theology, St. Mary's College, Kansas, in 1941. He did advanced studies at St. Stanislaus Novitiate, Cleveland, in 1941-42 and at the University of Toronto 1942-43 and 1944-45.

He was instructor in classics, St. Louis University High School, 1935-37; instructor in education, Campion Summer School, Prairie du Chein, Wis., 1937-41; instructor in philosophy, St. Louis University 1943-47; and has been assistant professor of philosophy since 1947. He has been dean of the School of Philosophy and Science, St. Louis University, since 1943, and dean of the Graduate School since 1950.

Father Henle is a member of the American Catholic Philosophical Association and was chairman of the committee on research of that organization 1949-50. He is also a member of the American Philosophical Society and is president of the Missouri State Philosophical Association 1950-51.

He was editor of *The Modern Schoolman* 1945-50. Among the books he has written are: *A Latin Grammer for High Schools*, 1937, revised edition, 1939; *First Year Latin*, 1937, revised edition, 1939; *Second Year Latin*, 1938, revised edition,

1939; *Third Year Latin,* 1940; *Fourth Year Latin,* 1942. He is a contributor to *The Modern Schoolman, The Historical Bulletin, The Classical Bulletin, America, Thought, The Catholic World, Jesuit Educational Quarterly, Bulletin of the National Catholic Educational Association.*

To the list of his writings the Aristotelian Society has the honor of adding *Method in Metaphysics.*

Method in Metaphysics

Method in Metaphysics

SOME twenty-two years ago, the emi-
nent Pere Marechal opened a series of
lectures at the University of Louvain in
which he intended to deal with the prob-
lems of the transcendental value of metaphysics.[1] The crux of the problem he cry-
stallized in what he called the question of
the gate to metaphysics, that is to say, the
passage from sense knowledge to metaphysical knowledge strictly so-called. It
is with this problem that I am here con-
cerned. I do not intend to deal directly
with the question of the transcendental
applications of metaphysics but rather
with the crucial issue of its origin in human knowledge from sense experience.

I do not intend to give either a complete and total explanation or one that is

entirely new. Much of what I will say has already been discovered and said by those before me, notably by the patron of these lectures, Thomas Aquinas. But above all I am fearful of falling into the fallacy which I have called the fallacy of "only." It is a dangerous temptation to which most philosophers yield at some point or other, to mistake some positive discovery or explanation for a total explanation—to say, for example, that because they have found one method of knowledge which is valid and intelligible, it is the only method of knowledge. Whenever we insert an "only" in a statement it becomes really two statements, one positive and the other negative. If we say, for example, "the only way to travel from Saint Louis to Milwaukee is by train," we are saying first that we can travel from Saint Louis to Milwaukee by train, which is obviously true, and secondly, that there is no other way we can travel from Saint Louis to Milwaukee, which is obviously false.

Moreover, while it is quite possible to prove the positive element in such a composite statement it is extremely difficult to prove a negative statement which almost has the force of a universal exclusion. This is the error of those who say, for example, that only the scientific method can yield valid knowledge or that only one type of science is true science.

Nor will I pretend to give an explanation which will constitute a "system" in the meaning which that term has acquired in modern thought. A system pretends to be complete and closed, and to be complete and closed a body of thought must have achieved an exhaustive transcription of its object into intelligible expression. For the philosopher whose object is the intelligibility of the whole of the real such a pretension would be equivalent to the deification of his own mind. Consequently any philosophical explanation, however sound and certain its positive elements may be, must remain open to deepening insight and the advancing conquest of reality. I hope that I shall be able to indicate at least how those discoveries and formulations which constitute the definitive contribution of historical Thomism to philosophy will remain within the framework of my proposed explanation.

I shall try therefore to avoid fallacious exclusion as well as specious and oversimplified completeness. While it is true that certain basic characters run through all our knowledge, there is, within the complexity of this knowledge, an almost endless variety of differences. The human mind has rich resources and a fecund creative power from which arise the astonishing devices and means—the metaphors, theories, abstractions, correlations, concepts, constructs, and so forth—by which it attempts to understand and control reality. A vast field of investigation lies open here which the Thomists have perhaps cultivated with too little effort. It may be that our failure here explains in

part why there is so little Thomistic contribution to the theory of art, or of
rhetoric, to the philosophy of history and
to the explanation of post-Renaissance
science.

Now when a science puts forth a claim
to be both an independent science and a
science of the real, this claim must be jus-
tified by establishing an immediate source
of data which is proper to this science and
not open to any other science or discipline. If metaphysics then is an independent, self-constituted science of the real,
there must be a point at which it is in a
privileged contact with reality and at
which it takes its origin. This moment
which I thus designate as a necessary
moment in the construction of any independent science of the real, I shall call
experiential for it is from human experience that metaphysics must draw its sus-
tenance.[2] *Our problem may be now described as that of the experiential moment
of metaphysics.*

For the purposes of the present discussion I shall make two presuppositions.

While a conscious study of method may precede a science in its pedagogical presentation, logically and historically, reflection on method follows at least the partial constitution of a science. I have therefore been able to limit my problem to a question of method because I am convinced that a body of valid metaphysical knowledge is in existence and may serve as a laboratory specimen for our investigation. I am presupposing that there is such a metaphysics which is, as a matter of fact, different from the body of knowledge in any other science and which is, moreover, not distilled from other sciences by any process of super generalization or universal analysis. The metaphysics to which I refer is existential Thomism, the metaphysics of being (*ens*) and existential act (*esse*).[3] At the point where this investigation begins, the problem of the possibility of metaphysics is, as a simple matter of given fact, already solved. Yet, though a valid metaphysics is given, it is neither whole or complete now nor will it ever constitute a closed and circumscribed system to which no addition can be made or in which no further depth is possible.

The existence of a valid metaphysics is then the first presupposition. It must be pointed out, however, that this is not a mere assumption. Thomistic existential metaphysics contains its own evidence and its own justification, though the examination of that evidence does not fall within the limits of this discussion.

Secondly, I do not intend to be led astray by the so-called "critical" problem, that mirage of speculation which has led so many modern philosophers to die of intellectual thirst in the arid desert of epistemology. I accept as certain that knowledge can be and, as a matter of fact, often is a knowledge of things as they are and of things which are. I do not presuppose for one moment that knowledge is a platonic vision of reality, that the intellectual object or even the sense object is given whole and entire, actuated, that is, in the order of knowledge, independently of the faculties which we possess and the modes of knowing which are ours. But to admit that knowledge involves subjective limitations is not to deny the massive fact, the common intuition, the objective evidence, that to know is to know something, and that in the first instance, to know is to know some sensible thing. Consequently, in what I have to say, it is presupposed that realism in a large sense is a sound philosophical position, though it is not to be understood as a naive realism or as the absolute realism of Plato. The basic position is that of a true realism that can find objectivity within human knowledge, an objectivity which is *per se* independent of the subjective modifications which make knowledge possible as well as of the emotions and other factors which may, indirectly, affect our knowledge. The validity of realism is therefore the second presupposition, though this, like the previous one, is no mere assumption or hypothesis.[4]

The problem before us can now be stated thus: *What is the experiential genesis of Thomistic existential metaphysics, viewed as an independent science of the real.*

We are therefore investigating the experiential moment of a certain kind of knowledge. Unfortunately the discussion cannot be conducted on so narrow a basis. It is necessary first to understand intellectual knowledge and its genesis in a more universal way before we can grasp this particular type. We must examine knowledge in itself.

Here a number of different approaches are ready at hand. Experimental psychology—or perhaps we should say experimental psychologies—use various indirect approaches: Intelligence, knowing and knowledge are measured and their manifestations correlated among themselves or with accompanying processes, neurological, physiological, and so forth. Knowledge is treated simply as a fact and the mystery of its nature abstracted from. Sometimes it is reduced to categories of physical processes (e.g. "reaction to environment") which methodically obscure what is peculiar to it. Because of the great variety of methods, it is difficult to characterize the whole body of experimental psychologies; yet, in the main, the approaches are "indirect" and leave the nature of knowledge in itself untouched.

For our purposes, it is necessary to study the unique and specific and, even mysterious, nature of knowledge as such, to grasp it in its own peculiar intelligibility. The approach must be direct, though we are confronted by an ultimate and almost inexpressible reality. The method must therefore be a philosophical one.[5]

Yet even philosophers have handled the nature of knowledge in different—and nonetheless—legitimate ways. The philosophy of knowledge being a direct science of a nature and hence ontological in character allows easily of a metaphysical prolongation. Those whose minds are peculiarly adapted to metaphysical consideration pass rapidly to this stage of philosophical explanation. Knowing and knowledge are viewed at this point as a kind of becoming and of being. Thus arises the strangely exhilarating theory of the *esse intentionale*, the order of intentential being and becoming.[6] While the uniqueness of knowledge does not disappear when it is thus translated into terms and conceptions (*esse*, act, etc.) which are proper to metaphysics, yet this way of understanding knowledge is not the simple and concrete view of its nature as given. The introduction of these higher and deeper insights of the metaphysician, while fruitful and valid, often tends to obscure the concrete peculiarity of the data to which they are being applied.

This metaphysical approach is, therefore, not the one we need here, however magnificent the sight to which it leads. We are interested in precisely the concrete richness of knowing in its own immediate and direct intelligibility.

Another traditional part of "rational psychology" (or "philosophy of man") has to do with the analysis of knowledge in terms of its efficient causes. The analysis begins with facts of experience in the order of knowledge. It requires a certain moderate measure of intelligent introspection to discover within consciousness, as moments or elements, of our knowing, the sense image and the concept. It is quite easy to become aware of the elaborated sense-presentation of an object; somewhat less easy to identify the concept of an object. Yet the concept was historically one of the earliest discoveries in the theory of knowledge; Socrates and Plato clearly identified it and distinguished it from the sense data, though neither of them was fully aware of what he had discovered. Aristotle further examined conceptual knowledge and laid down some of its definitive characteristics. Since then consideration of the concept has rarely been absent from philosophical discussion.

Because of the ease with which the image and the concept can be recognized and distinguished, Thomistic rational psychology has taken them for a starting point. Both image and concept stand out in the fluid processes of our knowing as clear-cut and formed terms; consequently in using them, Thomists have concentrated attention on the terms rather than on the processes of knowing. Taking certain characteristics (e.g., particular—universal; concrete—abstract) of image and concept, their natures are sharply and specifically distinguished, the one is found to be material, the other spiritual. The question of their genesis is now placed in the order of efficient causality, within which the whole elaborate structure of agent and possible intellect, and of the *species im-pressa* is set up. When the line of causality is followed according to this analysis, at only two points does it necessarily fall within consciousness. It begins with the elaborated sense presentation—the phantasm—which is discovered in consciousness and terminates at the fully-formed concept, the *verbum,* which is also consciously possessed. In between, the process, as far as this argument goes, is wholly below the level of consciousness and consequently only virtually in the order of knowledge as such.[7]

This reduction of knowing to its underlying efficient causes is of course valid and philosophically necessary, but there is a strong tendency at this point to commit the error of the "exclusive only." We so stress this part of the analysis that we are tempted to say that this is the whole story of the genesis of intellectual knowledge and the only causation to be considered. If we do so however, several very inconvenient results follow. By resting our case so exclusively on a "formed" result of intellectual activity—a "term"— namely the *verbum, "cogitatio formata,"* the fact of a process of formation is overlooked and a certain artificial cleavage introduced into our consciousness. By relating this term to a set of ontological and fundamentally general principles of activity, we give the impression of a certain mechanical rigidity little in keeping with the plasticity and mobility of our intellectual experience. There are other insufficiencies, some of which will appear in the course of the discussion, but at the moment it is more important to return to the main line of our argument.

The kind of investigation which I am proposing can now be described more closely. The approaches of the experimental psychologists fail us because they are extrinsic to the very nature of knowledge itself. The metaphysical consideration of knowledge does not reveal the immediately perceived unique character of knowledge but, presupposing this, moves on a more profound and generalized plane. The causal analysis rests mainly upon the material and spiritual character of the image and the concept and these characteristics are ontological rather than noetic characteristics. Having selected from directly perceived evidence these convenient facts and characteristics, it leaves the order of knowledge itself to establish ontological principles of operation.

The consideration we must employ must be centered on the immediately perceivable nature of knowing and knowledge. Our own knowing lies open, in its process and products, to immediate introspection and reflection. Hence, to remain wholly within the order of knowledge we must remain within consciousness where alone knowledge is formally present and discoverable.[8] The reflection needed is not a hasty glance sufficient to identify a *fact*;

it must be contemplative in character, a gaze concentrated and held steady until we penetrate the *nature* of knowing. We may then describe our procedure as a study of knowledge as such in its own unique and directly perceivable "intelligibility."

The introduction of the word "intelligibility" points up a seeming paradox in our procedure and at the same time leads directly to our next problem. We are attempting to achieve a knowledge of knowledge and are so led to speak of the intelligibility of intelligibility. But, however cumbersome such expressions may be and however verbally puzzling, there exists no real difficulty, since we are capable of intellectual reflection, in which knowledge is, in a sense, transparent to itself. All confusion can be avoided if we remember that "intelligibility" appears at two different levels in our discussion.

Intellectual knowledge involves an object (since knowledge is always knowledge *of*) and this object must be intelligible.[9] Consequently to understand knowledge, we must understand "intelligibility." Thus intelligibility is part of the subject matter of our investigation in which we must therefore inquire "What is intelligibility?" This is the first level at which intelligibility is involved.

Our approach to the problem of knowledge and intelligibility, as has been indicated, is direct and immediate, that is we are inquiring into intelligibility under the aspect of its intelligible nature. Thus at this second level, intelligibility is a formal constituent of the viewpoint from which we are considering knowledge.

For a proper understanding of both of these levels we must now attempt to understand what intelligibility means.

Considerable time must be devoted to this attempt for precisely here, both extreme rationalism and sensism have conspired to conceal "intelligibility" from the view of modern philosopher. We are at a point of crucial disagreement, and of irrevocable choices. "Choose" says the philosophical Queen; a fatal choice will be avenged by philosophy's own inexorable Furies.[10] Our method will imply an appeal to the immediate intellectual experience of each man and must amount to a pointing out through examples, rather than a description in alien terms, for we are up against a unique and ultimate reality that can be compared justly to nothing else in the world.

The obvious dialectical definition of understanding (*intelligere*) and the intelligible in terms of each other is thus of no service, for it is meaningless without an awareness of the immediate experience in which the two are found together. We can compare them in the line of act and potency, explain them in terms of general categories, as object and subject, as being or becoming, or illumine them by metaphors, scientific or literary, drawn from sight and the visible, from light and image, but the peculiar reality of intellection and intelligibility escapes all these devices and remains in its own nature unique and ultimate.

The difficulty is increased by the distortions which philosophy and scientific theory have introduced into the whole question of intelligence and its operations. Philosophical reflection and analysis has, in many cases, proceeded as though there were, in the whole of man's conscious activity or in large areas of it, no such thing as intelligibility.[11] I do not mean to say that any thinker has been able to work without intelligibility, but I do mean that many thinkers have excluded it in whole or in part from their formal theoretical explanations, or have misinterpreted and disfigured it. It goes without saying that any crude materialist would do so. An example of an attempt to explain knowledge without considering either intellection or intelligibility is the naturalistic theory of Ralph Barton Perry.[12] To one who practiced intellectual reflection, Professor Perry's explanation appears incredible, an amazing feat of sustained ignoring—and the theory can only be seriously regarded when one remembers the theoretical presuppositions which entail such an explanation. The history of philosophy offers many examples. To find Berkeley reducing the intelligibility of concepts to sense images in the very example in which he is unmistakably describing the fact of an understanding of a common nature is at least amazing.[13] It is as though a detective were to establish the non-existence of a murderer by the very argument in which he clearly identifies and convicts a living criminal.

In order to capture intelligibility in the moment of its experiential presentation the practice of intellectual reflection to an uncommon degree is therefore requisite, accompanied by an ascetic abstention from obscuring theories and theoretical interpretations. Intellection and intelligi-

bility are pervasive in our conscious living, yet, as Chesterton has said, it is the
vast and obvious thing that a man over-
looks. A man may gaze at grass in safety
ninety-nine times; the hundredth time he
may see at last that grass is green!

Let us suppose a person who has no
experience and no knowledge of rectangularity, a person to whom both the word
"rectangularity" and the content which it
expresses are as yet unknown. In order to
induce in him the knowledge of "rectangularity," I present to him a rectangular
card. The card enters his consciousness in
the elaborated phantasm (the unified
sense presentation). A variety of characters are, of course, here re-presented for
the card has a certain roughness or
smoothness, a definite color, size and lo-
cation. By a series of rhetorical elimina-
tions and "pointings" I focus the person's
intellectual attention on the shape of the
card. He not only senses the shape, he
intellectually sees the peculiar type of

shape which I am designating as rectangularity. He sees it thus in the card itself and in the re-presentation of the card in the phantasm which is a transparent revelation of the card itself. The very moment in which he sees the rectangularity, he begins to assimilate it intellectually, he begins to understand what is meant by rectangularity, to possess this meaning and to express it to himself in a concept. The full actualization of this understanding (intellection) is reached only when he manages to express it in an articulated definition. There is nothing unusual about this experience; it is the common experience of learning from sense presentation of real objects. The understanding which begins with the first active moment of seeing the rectangularity in the card and reaches its first completion in a conceptual definition is what we mean by intellection. It is contemporaneous with the sensible experience though different from it. Reflecting upon it we see that it can be called an active assimilation of the rectangularity of the card, an expression in intellectual knowledge of the same rectangularity, an insight into the presentation of sense and the experienced card. The rectangularity in turn is called intelligible because it can be thus the object of intellection. Now, just as the act of intellection reveals in itself a continuous series of stages, so does the intelligibility of the object. There is the point before the card is presented; there is here no act of intellection with regard to rectangularity; the card is presented and attention focused, the intellection begins by an active insight stimulated by the sense re-presentation; it reaches perfection only when the rectangularity *of the card* is expressed by the intellect to itself and possessed in a definition transparently present to intellectual consciousness.

So also with the rectangularity *of the card*. Before the card is presented, it is not understood but it can be understood

—for it is the rectangularity of the card that the intellect will assimilate. Though *intelligible,* (can be understood) at this point the card is not within the order of intellectual knowledge at all; hence it is said to be potentially intelligible. When it is presented in sense experience, it enters the field of knowledge; it can be understood, but it is still not within the order of intellectual knowledge, it is still potentially intelligible and it is still the intelligibility *of the card* which is being "carried" and re-presented by the phantasm. Only when the rectangularity begins to be "seen" by intelligence does it move into intellectual knowledge, and only when it is expressed in a concept is it wholly actuated within intellectual understanding. At this point therefore the rectangularity *of the card* is understood and actually intelligible.

In knowing the rectangularity of the card, we see that its intelligibility is not another reality or character super-added to rectangularity; it is the rectangularity itself. The rectangularity is a reality in the card and, to exactly the same extent, an intelligibility of the card. At every stage in the process so experienced, it is the intelligibility *of the card* which is in question, and in the final stage, completed in a direct existential judgment, when we say "This card is rectangular," it is the real rectangular card which is understood, expressed and asserted.

This instance reveals to reflection the meaning of intellection and intelligibility. It has the additional advantage of exposing the stages in which an intelligibility may exist as potentially intelligible, actually intelligible and actually understood. Moreover it is the type of intellection which is basic in human knowledge for it begins with sense data and moves to pure intellection without ever cutting itself, epistemologically, from the concrete object.

Yet the same active power of insight is found in many different processes. We might take a case in which we are no longer dealing with the intelligibility presented by a sense phantasm. Whenever the intellect follows a line of reasoning and constructs a formal syllogism in which it assents to a conclusion because it sees it flowing from or involved in two premises, the intellect perceives a relationship which exists between the premises and the conclusion. The perception of this relationship is an understanding, an *intelligere*. The relationship itself, since it can be perceived in this peculiar intellectual way, is said to be intelligible. It is actually intelligible because it does not have to be transferred from a buried sort of existence in sense data to the actualization of pure intellectual knowledge but can be immediately perceived as soon as the premises are set up. Given the premises, the mind perceives the necessary connections and assents to the conclusion. The intelligibility of the connection is immediately seen, and, again, this character of intelligibility is not simply superadded to the relationship but is identical with it in so far as the relationship is, in its very nature, transparent to conscious intelligence.

These instances should suffice to indicate where intelligibility is to be found in experience and how contemplation of it is to be carried on. I do not mean to say that the account just given does not raise many questions and difficulties. Much less would I pretend that any one who has been accustomed to approach knowledge through the selective abstractions and indirections of experimental psychology or through the obfuscating theories of non-realistic or anti-intellectual philosophies will readily perceive the content of this experience or its meaning and bearing.

However, though these instances would suffice for our immediate purpose, I intend to treat yet another case, for this special case, besides emphasizing the nature of intelligibility, will supply a necessary groundwork for later developments.

Let us suppose again that I am holding up a card before your eyes. I then draw a line dividing the card. The card, I tell you, with reference to this division is called "the whole," the divisions as divisions are called "parts." I point out that I could indicate parts by drawing complete lines anywhere on the surface. By a process similar to that in the case of rectangularity, I thus induce an understanding of "whole" and "part" in a quantitative sense. As in the previous case, you can continue to contemplate the "whole" and the "parts" *in the card.* As you continue to do so, the question is put, "Is this whole greater than any part I indicate?" Yes. "Is it in the nature of the case that it must be so?" Yes. Observe the card. Observe the "whole" and the "parts." It is immediately obvious *in the card* that the whole card must be larger than any indicated part.

Not only is the intelligibility of "whole," "part," "larger" intellectually perceived in the card itself but *the intelligible necessity of the relationship is likewise seen in the card itself.* This may go against the doctrinal grain of all those who have been accustomed to think of the necessity of principles as involving some *a priori* element or as being derived from conceptual analysis. I would suggest that at no point have preconceptions more thoroughly obscured the true state of the case.[14] The necessity is first of all an intelligible ontological necessity; the necessity is in the reality experienced; it is an intelligible necessity just as rectangularity was an intelligible modification of the card. Consequently, it can be and is directly understood in the sense-experienced data, in the reality itself. Because it is found in reality and there understood, it can be expressed in knowledge. The necessity of the principle does not arise from intellect but from reality; necessity qualifies the expression in the order of knowledge because the necessity is ontological and being determines knowledge.

The necessity is already in the singular judgment as a *de jure* and not merely a *de facto* necessity. It requires only a reflection—that in fact adds nothing—to purify the proposition of accidental elements and express it as a principle of continuous quantity in general: "The whole is greater than any of its parts."

It will be recalled that instances of understanding were introduced here in order to guide intellectual reflection to the discovery of intellection and intelligibility. The central point in the instances is that peculiar activity which is understanding. If we have been able to recognize the existence and character of this activity, we now see how it permeates intellectual knowledge, no matter how diverse the mode of knowing or the things known.

Anything, therefore, which can be known intellectually, which can fall under intellectual activity may be designated as intelligible, whether potentially or actually. Intelligibility is not a character or reality added to the thing known; the thing as such can be known and its intelligibility is therefore, in the first instance, concretely identical with it. The thing however as knowable or as known can be re-presented in the order of knowledge; all the "carriers" or "expressions" of the knowable and the known are simply, in the first instance, expressions and carriers of the intelligibility *of a thing which is known.* Consequently, whether the intelligibility be on an ontological mode of being (as rectangularity) or a necessary ontological relationship (the whole is greater than any of its parts), it is always the intelligibility found in the real order that continues to be understood and reflected upon in intellectual operations.

Two further points must be noted here. The reflective contemplation and the analysis (of experiential data, not of concepts) we have just conducted leads to the broadest possible extension of meaning for the term intelligible: indeed, a great deal of our remaining task will be taken up by filling in the matters to which it can be applied and exploring the diversity of intellection.

Though the instances were introduced to illustrate intelligibility, a review of our discussion will reveal that we have actually described in the first and second case the process of induction through insight. We maintained ourselves strictly within a noetic consideration, contrasting the known and knowing, the intelligible and intellection. When an intelligibility is brought to full act, in the pure intellectual state, if it contains an understood ontological necessity, this necessity is seen to be potentially multiple to the exact extent to which the intelligibility in which it is, is potentially multiple. That is to say, if the ontological intelligibility is capable of being in other instances, the understanding of that precise intelligibility in pure intelligible form will be seen, on reflection, to be universal; that is, it can be used as a means of understanding and expressing further instances.

Certain important conclusions can be drawn here: 1) The opposition of knowledge and the known is not an opposition of thing and thing, nor of particular and universal but of thing and that thing's actually grasped intelligibility. 2) Universality is not a *per se* characteristic of knowledge as such; it attaches to certain kinds of human knowledge because of the conditions, subjective and objective, under which human knowledge takes place. 3) Consequently, to state the problem of knowledge as primarily involving a tension of individuality and universality or of contingency and necessity is to set up a pseudo-problem and to repeat both the Platonic and the Kantian error. In other words the problem of induction is fundamentally solved as soon as the fact and nature of inductive insight, that is of the movement of intelligibility from a potential to an actual state within intellectual knowledge, is discovered and realized. The reflection we conducted above can bring us to this discovery and, slowly indeed, to this realization.

The facts which we have reviewed would be impossible if there were a sharp and absolute break between sense and intellect. The openness of sense to the active insight of intelligence is a central and often overlooked fact. The expression "potentially intelligible" designates the sense re-presentation as it thus falls under the activity of intellect. The Thomistic doctrine of potential intelligibility is therefore not a theory resulting from an *a priori* application of act and potency but is the expression of immediately observed facts.

The moment a sensible object enters consciousness through its re-presentation in the phantasm it falls within intellectual awareness. The phantasm, epistemologically speaking, initiates the activity of intellectual knowledge and the moment of attention and awareness is the first moment of the causality of sense with reference to intellectual knowledge. *The phantasm is object of awareness for the intellect and, qua object, a mover.*[15]

All this is merely an explication of the content of our previous analysis. Yet it will appear to many Thomists to be an intolerable paradox. The limited analytic procedure by which phantasm and concept are sharply distinguished and related to independent and essentially diverse faculties tends to obscure the vital unity of sense and intellect. Sense and intellect are, of course, essentially diverse, and the sense faculties cannot be the efficient cause or seat of concepts. Yet experience reveals that we are intellectually aware of the phantasm and that there is a conscious continuity within the integral act of human knowing.

The facts may be approached from another angle. Thomistic philosophers, in establishing the unity of man, have frequently made use of the immediately perceived unity of consciousness. Our experience does not reveal two distinct consciousnesses, each cabined, cribbed and confined in itself. Sense consciousness and intellectual consciousness may be formally diverse but they are experientially conjoined; intellectual awareness permeates all our conscious life.

Doubtless, unity of consciousness is evidence of a unity of substance; the ontological ground must be found in one substance. Boswell may cling as closely as he wishes, pad and pencil in hand, to Samuel Johnson, yet his sense consciousness can never merge with the intellectual consciousness of his idol and master. The argument is metaphysically ineluctable— but what is frequently overlooked is that the very evidence for it is a *unity at the level of operation,* the permeation of the whole of consciousness by intellectual awareness. The self-aware light of intelligence is not focused solely on the limited area of concepts or of judgments, but spreads through the more obscure places of sensation and emotion.

If one finds it difficult to discover this fact in conscious experience, we might point it up by asking how we can intellectually assert the distinctive characteristics of the phantasm and rationally conclude to its formal diversity from the concept? Are not these characters—and consequently the phantasm itself—immediately open to intellectual reflection?

The phantasm therefore is itself an object of intellectual awareness. As such, it re-presents to intellectual insight the ontological reality known through it; that is, it carries the potential intelligibility of that reality. As soon as it becomes object of intellectual awareness and attention, it is engaged in the causality of knowledge. Yet, though it is an intelligible object, it is not a wholly satisfactory object; intellect cannot grasp its intelligibility purely and spiritually until, as we have pointed out before, it possesses this intelligibility in a pure intellectual and intelligibly transparent way. The potential intelligibility of the object, both thing re-presented and phantasm, must be moved to the actual intelligibility of pure intelligence. Again, the fact of a process within consciousness is indicated.

If we review the instances of "rectangularity" and the principle of "whole and part," we see that the process begins precisely with an intellectual "looking," a contemplation of the sense data in which there is a growing understanding, a progressive and active assimilation of intelligibility.[16] In many cases the process is relatively simple and rapid, in others there is definitely an effort, a conscious effort to understand and to express. The effort to express what is seen in the sense re-presentation is, in many cases, the effort to form a concept and to articulate a definition.

I should like to point out again that, if the analysis of knowledge into its ontological efficient causes were the whole story, the process and effort within consciousness (and within the formal order of knowledge) would be wholly unintelligible, for the transition from phantasm to concept or definition would lie below the level of consciousness. Experience reveals that this latter is not the true account.

There is another experience to which we can appeal to bring out the point that I am making. There are two very clear ways in which conceptual knowledge of any object may be increased. We can learn for example that this is a man. We can extend this knowledge by discovering that man is rational. We can further extend it by discovering and stating that he is an animal. In this extension of our understanding of man we are expressing distinct intelligibilities to which logicians often refer as notes. These notes can be held apart in distinct concepts or they can be brought together in a composite concept. They can be thought of as simple objects of the understanding or they can be used as predicates, but the point is that the extension of knowledge here is *by way of addition of distinct intelligibilities or notes.*[17]

The extension of knowledge in the way just described obviously involves an increase in distinct intelligibilities within the order of quiddity. There is, however, another way in which knowledge may be extended. This way may be characterized, in opposition to the previous type just described, as a deepening of insight. The concept or the intelligible note or the pure expression of intelligibility is never exhaustive and may consequently vary not only between different individuals but also within the development of any single individual's knowledge.[18] It is a common experience of those who have engaged in intellectual work or study to find that with increased experience, after viewing, for example, a number of divergent instances of the same intelligibility or after constructing in the imagination metaphors or symbols of the same intelligibility, there is an increase of understanding so that a person says, "Now I see what that meant" or "Now I appreciate the full meaning of that." For example, the very experience of intellectual life itself constantly adds to our understanding of the intelligibility expressed by the word "rational" in the definition of man. In this type of extension of knowledge there is no question of an added note, no question of a new intelligibility. Consequently, we frequently find ourselves unable to express the increased depth by the simple addition of a new term. It becomes necessary for us to indulge in an indirect rhetorical or psychological method, utilizing sense experiences and metaphors and so forth, in order to bring home to anyone the new understanding which we ourselves have achieved and now enjoy. Clearly in this case there is a conscious relationship between the expression of the intelligibility in the concept and the experience of the sense data which gives rise to the deepening of understanding. The concept is not a mechanical expression of something which has appeared on a different level or in a different consciousness, but it is worked out and elaborated, it grows from the very intellectual contemplation of the sense data themselves.[19]

The importance of insight into the phantasm is pointed up also by another fact. Even after we have elaborated a concept, we find it necessary to return, as it were, to the phantasm, to re-embody the intelligibility in a sense presentation in order to understand fully the intelligibility expressed. In the same way, when attempting to understand something, we often create phantasms in which to read the intelligibility we are trying to grasp.[20]

From these few indications and this brief review of cognitive experience we find: 1) that the phantasm is an object of intellectual awareness, 2) that as such it initiates the active movement of intelligence, 3) that it is potentially intelligible in the order of conceptual intelligibility, 4) that as object of awareness and as potentially intelligible it is object also of an active insight through which we read, with varying depth and fullness, the intelligibility it contains and as a result of which we express, with varying degrees of effort, its intelligibility in a pure conceptual state. The intellect, using a concept as a formal *signum quo*, returns to the sense, therein to contemplate the intelligibility understood through the concept—at this point knowledge is rich, real, accurate.[21]

If all this is true, the initial ontological insights are all dependent upon sense, in the first instance, and derivative from it, not by argumentation or inference but by

immediate insight.[22] It follows that the
fundamental concepts are neither given *a
priori* in the intellect, nor formed from
sense experience by a quasi-automatic
"natural abstraction" which guarantees
their exhaustive and perfect character and
eliminates contemplation and effort. If
this is true in general, it is eminently true
of that most realistic, most ontological of
all the sciences, metaphysics. Its content,
its intelligible necessities must be drawn
in the first instance from sense data by inductive insight.[23] Its method in origin
must therefore be inductive, not deduc-
tive. Since the intelligibilities so derived
are not exhaustive and never complete,
the metaphysician must at every step re-
sort to the sense data, must continue to
employ inductive insight at every point
where his science rests boldly on the real.[24]

With some few exceptions what I have
said up to this point would seem to presuppose that concepts express all that insight can discover in sense-presented real-

ity and that human knowledge reaches its fullness and final perfection in conceptual knowledge. Our next investigations will show that this is not so.

Let us take the direct judgment "This card is rectangular." Several points must be noted:

1. We are talking about and thinking about a thing, an actually existing being. We are not talking about concepts, nor about the content of concepts *qua* conceptual content, nor about phantasms. The judgment is and expresses knowledge of reality; the epistemological term of this act of knowledge is the existing rectangular card. The psychological and/or epistemological media are here transparent in the order of knowledge; in technical terms, they here function as pure formal signs. There is a vital connection within the order of knowl-

edge between this judgment and the card.

2. The judgment is itself an intellectual act. It is formally constituted and unified by an intellectual assent, an affirmation which englobes within intellectual vision and acceptance all the knowledge expressed in the judgment, whether this knowledge is wholly actuated in the intelligible order or not.

3. According to the causal analysis of knowledge, the ontological efficient cause of the act of judgment is the intellect itself. To seek the cause however *within the order of knowledge itself*, the true cognitional cause, is to seek the evidence upon which the judicial assent rests. But to seek this evidence in the case of a direct judgment like "This card is rectangular" is to ask for the source of the knowledge.

What is the complete knowledge expressed in the judgment?

In this judgment there are quidditive conceptual elements which can be considered separately as actual intelligibilities, the quiddity of "card" and the quiddity of "rectangularity." Conceptualized in their actual intelligibilities, these elements are knowledge of formal constituents and reveal the characteristics of all such knowledge. They are abstracted from the concrete "here and now" and from existence. In such cases the intellect has assimilated itself to the formal nature of the thing known, living its life by sharing the determination of its form, but according to its own spiritual mode.[25]

But besides these elements the judgment englobes a knowledge of the concrete individual, for it is not merely "card," it is "*this* card" that is known and expressed in the intellectual act which is the judgment. While there is no opposition between the abstract form "card" and its individualization in this card, the concept neither contains nor expresses the individual. This is to say that the concrete individual cannot be distilled into pure intelligibility. On this point experience is definitive, and this has been rather consistently recognized throughout the Thomistic traditon. Yet, it is part of the intelligibility carried by the phantasm, read there by the intellect and expressed in the judgment. Hence, the intelligence can only bear upon an individual as it is presented or re-presented in sense. A vital operational continuity (*continuatio*) of sense and intellect is thus necessary for the concrete existential judgment.[26]

The same results may be obtained by a consideration of concrete time[27] and place, but above all, by a consideration of concrete existence. Reflection on pure conceptual intelligibility reveals its neutrality with regard to being; it expresses the *rationes* of things, not their existence. Or again, among material things only the concrete individual exercises the act of existence; concepts, because of their very mode, abstract from the material individual. It is equally impossible to express an existing material individual in a concept and to *derive* actual existence from concepts.[28]

Consequently, the concrete existential judgment requires wider and deeper insight into the phantasm, quite independently of the distillation of concepts. Actual existence cannot be expressed in conceptual intelligibility; only a vital *continuatio* between intellect and sense can underlie the judgment expressing it. Neither the concrete individual nor its act of existence is in the order of form. The intellect assimilates itself to the existing thing through the exercise of a corresponding act within the order of knowledge, that is in a vital act of judgment in which the intellect lives the life of the thing in the "is"—no longer a colorless copula but objectivated and energized by assent through intellectual insight and transparently expressing the *existing* thing.

The intelligibilities and intelligible necessities which are expressed in the direct existential judgment are therefore known in the object and carried by the phantasm. The formal intelligibilities and formal necessities do not however cover the whole of this knowledge and consequently quidditative concepts are inadequate as expression of it. Intelligibility appears in two orders, that of form or essence and that of *esse,* the act of existence. Our intellectual knowledge overflows the limits of conceptualization and is fully grasped only in the judgment.

Let us turn then to metaphysics. The basic insight and intelligibility of Thomistic existential metaphysics is that of the *esse,* the act of existence. Metaphysics does not ignore the order of essence or the total structure of beings, but all its contemplation, all its effort to understand is carried on in the light of this act, *esse.*

By this metaphysics is differentiated from all other sciences, for *esse* as intelligible does not command the formal considerations of any other science. By the same token, metaphysics is a philosophical science, since it deals with direct intelligibilities.

The experiential moment of metaphysics is therefore the moment of vital contact with reality in direct existential judgments. The primary necessities and insights of metaphysics are not deduced from concepts, nor added by *a priori* forms in the mind but are already contained in the existential judgments we constantly make.[29]

Yet to possess this knowledge in a series of such judgments is not to be a metaphysician or to possess a metaphysics. The necessities are there in the object known, in the phantasm, in the judgment; the intelligibilities are there. But in the direct judgment they are not possessed in their pure intelligibility nor in their full depth. By what process can this knowledge be moved from a stage of direct understanding to a stage of full explicit possession, without adding thereby to the knowledge itself any intrinsic modification? Since knowledge is transparent to itself and subject to self-direction the means lie ready to hand in reflection. We have already seen in the case of the principle "The whole is greater than any of its parts," an instance of the operation of reflection in achieving a scientific status for knowledge of what is seen in the object. A similar procedure is necessary here. Reflection must be exercised upon the knowledge expressed in the judgment (not upon the judgment as a psychological act or a *form* of knowing) for two purposes: 1) to *direct* and focus contemplation of the reality itself with which the judgment is in living contact; 2) to order the intelligibilities of the judgment and understand them in their purity. The first is a process of deepening insight, a nourishing and enriching of the mind with the strong food of reality; the second lifts the knowledge to the level of consciously possessed intelligibility, that is, to the level of philosophical science. There must be a continuous movement between the two phases; thus metaphysics becomes ever deeper, ever more firmly grasped.

Metaphysics therefore cannot proceed by analyzing concepts. There are, in the first place, no concepts clear and exhaustive after the Cartesian pattern either given initially or infallibly produced by an automatic abstraction of the mind. Moreover, even given such concepts, existence, either concrete or purely intelligible, could never be derived from them. A metaphysics of conceptual analysis could never extend roots into the rich soil of reality.[30]

Nor can metaphysics arise from a reflection upon the forms of knowing, since as forms they would be empty of real content; the contact with reality would not be maintained.

Metaphysics must therefore be derived from experience, through a constantly purifying reflection. Nor does this refer to a single starting-point; the fundamental necessities and intelligibilities with which metaphysics deals and on which it builds must be continually discovered in concrete experience.

We can once more illustrate by briefly examining a basic principle—that well-worn, much-maligned principle of contradiction. Often it is presented as an inference from the concept of being or as primarily a law of thought. Sometimes we do think and speak as though it were a pattern laid up in an intellectual heaven with which we must force things to agree or as though it were a mental mold by which neutral and fluid experience must be shaped and formed. But, as a matter of fact, its intelligibility is present in the first and in any direct existential judgment.

Any uneducated person recognizes the concrete intelligibility and necessity of the principle and rejects as absurd and laughable any suggested instance of its violation. The principle is, in fact, merely a recognition of the necessity of being in a given act of existence. "When Socrates sits, he sits with necessity." Reflection upon this intelligibility merely releases it in its purity, so that the scientific statement of the principle is an intelligible transcription of the necessities of concrete *esse*.

The example of the principle of contradiction is introduced here to supplement and recall the example of the principle "The whole is greater than any of its parts." Both can be seen, on reflection, to illustrate induction through intellectual insight. But the principle of contradiction expresses an intelligible necessity of the *act of existence* while the other principle is limited to the order of form and quiddity. Once we have discovered that intelligibility extends beyond quiddities and conceptualization, it becomes evident that metaphysical principles and insights depend likewise upon an induction through insight. The illustration of the principle of contradiction serves merely to summarize all our results in a strictly metaphysical principle.

At the beginning of the discussion we placed our question as that of the origin of metaphysics from sense-experience. We were dealing with an existing valid and realistic metaphysics, the metaphysics of being and its act, *esse*. We then asked, with more precision, what the privileged experiential moment of this metaphysics was and by what method metaphysics was derived from this experiential moment.

We have discovered that the privileged experiential moment of metaphysics lies in the experience from which arise the concrete existential judgments which we all make; from this experience metaphysics is derived by induction through intellectual insight and a purifying reflection. The experiential moment is privileged in the sense that metaphysics keeps always in view the intelligibility of *esse,* while all the other sciences attend, by direct or indirect means, to quidditative intelligibilities and, at most, presuppose existence or treat it as a fact and not as an intelligibility. Moreover, the concrete and realistic character of metaphysics is evident, since its insights and principles are found directly in reality. Finally, its position at the peak of philosophical science is clearly validated, for it deals not merely with quidditative or formal intelligibilities but with the intelligibility of that most intimate and ultimate of acts, *esse,* in the light of which it and it alone considers all things.

NOTES

1. Maréchal, "Au seuil de la métaphysique: Abstraction ou intuition," *Revue Neo-scolastique*, vol. 31 (1929), pp. 27-52, 309-42.

2. I use the word "experiential" to designate a wider area than that covered by "experimental" or "empirical." These latter words have been appropriated to indicate the methods of physical science. If they are allowed to cover all the modes of immediate contact with reality, then there is no room for an independent philosophy and metaphysics. The positions would be determined by an assumption which, however widespread and currently respectable, remains a mere assumption. If metaphysics does not have an initial (and continuing) contact with concrete reality independently of the methods of so-called scientific methodology, then it cannot be an ontology, an independent science of being, but rather a meta-physics, a meta-mathematics, or some other sort of discipline at two removes from experience and subject to the limited sciences upon which it depends.

3. The best general view of Thomistic existentialism in English is to be found in Etienne Gilson, *Being and Some Philosophers* (Toronto: Pontifical Institute of Mediaeval Studies, 1949), chapter 5, pp. 154-89. See also, Gilson, *L'être et l'essence* (Paris: Vrin, 1948), *Le Thomisme,* (5th ed., Paris: Vrin, 1944), especially pp. 42-68; 497-523. Thomistic existentialism is, of course, profoundly opposed to the current existentialisms of Sartre, Jaspers, etc.

4. See Gilson, *Réalisme thomiste et critique de la connaissance* (Paris: Vrin, 1939); Maritain, "Le réalisme critique," in *Les Degrés du Savoir* (5th ed., Paris: Desclée, 1946), pp. 137-263. The remark of Gilson with regard to modern thought and Thomistic realism needs emphasis: "Hence in the first place we see that modern critics of scholasticism do not so much as suspect either the nature or the depth of the gulf that divides them from it." *The Spirit of Mediaeval Philosophy* (New York: Scribner's, 1940), p. 238.

5. The treatment here presupposes a distinction in methodology between the philosophical and the physical sciences. In the philosophical sciences ontological intelligibility

is dealt with directly; consequently contemplative insight and induction-through-insight are essential to philosophical method. In the physical sciences ontological intelligibility is not primary; indirect understanding and control of certain aspects of reality is achieved through constructs and induction-by-inference. Thus the concept of "mass" in physics is typical of the physical sciences; the understanding of the substantial unity of a living organism is typical of philosophy. Certain points of this distinction may be found, in a somewhat exaggerated form, in Ardley, *Aquinas and Kant* (New York: Longmans, 1950). See also Hawkins, "Induction and Hypothesis," *Casuality and Implication* (London: Sheed and Ward, 1937), pp. 107-22.

6. Cf. J. Maritain, *Les Degrés du Savoir*, pp. 215-30.

7. E.g. Remer, *Psychologia* (Westminster: Newman, 1942), pp. 134-96.

8. This procedure is in no sense to be confused with that of Descartes. Descartes begins within a *closed* consciousness wherein he finds *thought* and *ideas* and from which he must argue to external realities. In a true realism, reflective consciousness discovers

knowledge of *things* and finds itself in *immediate contact with reality.* This *knowing* must, however, be studied by reflective contemplation.

9. D. J. B. Hawkins, *The Criticism of Experience* (New York: Sheed and Ward, 1945), ch. 1, pp. 11-23.

10. Both Hume and pre-Kantian Rationalism agree in denying intelligibility to sense-given objects. Sensism uses this to destroy the entire order of intelligibility and with it all rational necessities. Rationalism asserts the independent and *a priori* character of thought. In either case reality as given is opaque to the eye of intelligence. See J. Maritain, *Réflexions sur l'intelligence* (Paris: Desclée, 1930), pp. 9-77. Maréchal, *Le point de départ de la métaphysique* (Paris: Alcan, 1923), Cahier II, pp. 179-85.

11. "Psychologists, following the biologists, who are themselves following the physicists, feel that at all costs they must be objective. Therefore they study man in a detached sort of way, as if they were not men themselves. Mr. Sidney Hook has seriously wondered (in *Education for Modern Man*) whether man is

intelligent. He says this is an empirical question on which considerable evidence has accumulated. One would think that Mr. Hook, having made the acquaintance of some men, would know whether they are intelligent or not. But no. Scientific reserve demands the cautious statement that "evidence has accumulated." But how does evidence accumulate? Does it lie around in a sort of dustpile, or does it accumulate in minds, and if so, don't the men have to be intelligent in order to take in the evidence? Perhaps it would not be too outrageously daring to conclude that "at least some men possess at least some intelligence." Mr. Hook might have come to this conclusion by contemplating himself. But here is the point—by the rules of the scientific game, he is not allowed to contemplate himself. To do so would not be objective. It would be subjective. It would be using *introspection,* a procedure which is regarded with the darkest suspicion by all true scientists." Anthony Standen, *Science Is a Sacred Cow* (New York: E. P. Dutton & Co., 1950), pp. 118-19.

12. Ralph Barton Perry, *Present Philosophical Tendencies* (New York: Longman's, 1919), pp. 271-328.

13.   Berkeley, *The Principles of Human Knowledge* (La Salle, Ill.: Open Court, 1940), "Introduction," pp. 14-19.

14.   Both extreme sensism and extreme rationalism agree in denying any intelligible necessity to the sense-presented object. Along with Kant, a great deal of modern thought has worked under this restrictive assumption. Cf. Kant, *Critique of Pure Reason*, tran. Smith (London: Macmillan, 1933), "Introduction," pp. 43-45; Smith, *A Commentary to Kant's 'Critique of Pure Reason'* (London: Macmillan, 1930), pp. xxxiii-xxxiv. The simple fact is that some necessities can be seen in the sense-experienced reality. The absolute opposition of contingent and necessary is not verified as between experience and intellectual knowledge. "Respondeo. Dicendum quod contingentia dupliciter possunt considerari. Uno modo, secundum quod contingentia sunt. Alio modo, secundum quod in eis aliquid necessitatis invenitur; *nihil enim est adeo contingens, quin in se aliquid necessarium habeat*. Sicut hoc ipsum quod est Socratem currere, in se quidem contingens est; sed habitudo cursus ad motum est necessaria;

necessarium enim est Socratem moveri, si currit." *Summa Theol.* I q. 86 a. 3.

15. For a fuller development of this point as it refers to conceptual knowledge, see B. Lonergan, S.J., "The Concept of *Verbum* in the Writings of St. Thomas Aquinas," *Theological Studies,* VII (1946), pp. 372-80, especially the valuable footnote on page 373.

16. "Unde intelligit quidem immaterialia, sed inspicit ea in aliquo materiali." *Contra Gentiles* II 73 (ed. Leonine vol. 13, p. 462.) ". . . finis autem potentiae intellectivae non est cognoscere phantasmata, sed cognoscere species intelligibiles, quas apprehendit a phantasmatibus, et in phantasmatibus secundum statum praesentis vitae." *Summa Theol.* III q. 11 a. 2 ad 1, (ed. Leonine vol. 11, p. 160.) ". . . Quando aliquis conatur aliquid intelligere, format sibi aliqua phantasmata per modum exemplorum, in quibus quasi inspiciat quod intelligere studet." *Summa Theol.* I q. 84 a. 7, (ed. Leonine vol. 5, p. 325.) . . . "Intellectus noster et abstrahit species intelligibiles a phantasmatibus, inquantum considerat naturas rerum in universali; et tamen intelligit eas in phantasmatibus," *Summa Theol.* I q. 85 a. 1 ad 5, (ed. Leonine vol. 5, p. 332.)" . . .

Non potest secundum eas (species intelligibiles) actu intelligere nisi convertendo se ad
phantasmata, in quibus species intelligibiles
intelligit, ut dicitur." *Summa Theol.* I q. 86
a. 1 (ed. Leonine vol. 5, p. 347.)

17. *Summa Theol.* I q. 85 a. 5.

18. *Summa Theol.* I q. 85 a. 7.

19. "The Scotist rejection of insight into phantasm necessarily reduced the act of understanding to seeing a nexus between concepts;
hence, while for Aquinas, understanding pre-
cedes conceptualization which is rational, for
Scotus, understanding is preceded by conceptualization which is a matter of metaphysical
mechanics. It is the latter position that gave
Kant the analytic judgments which he criti-
cized; and it is the real insufficiency of that
position which led Kant to assert his syn-
thetic *a priori* judgments; on the other hand,
the Aristotelian and the Thomist positions
both consider the Kantian assumption of
purely discursive intellect to be false and,
indeed, to be false, not as a point of theory,
but as a matter of fact." B. Lonergan, S.J.,
"The Concept of *Verbum* in the Writings of
St. Thomas Aquinas," *Theological Studies,*
VII (1946), p. 373, footnote.

20. "Quilibet in se ipso experiri potest, quod quando aliquis conatur aliquid intelligere, format sibi aliqua phantasmata per modum exemplorum, in quibus quasi inspiciat quod intelligere studet" St. Thomas, *Summa Theol.* I, q. 84 a. 7.

21. For a description of "formal sign," see J. Maritain, *Les Degrés du Savoir,* pp. 228-35.

22. "Non autem manifestantur nobis principia abstractorum, ex quibus demonstrationes in eis procedunt, nisi ex particularibus aliquibus, quae sensu percipimus. Puta ex hoc, quod videmus aliquod totum singulare sensibile, perducimur ad cognoscendum quid est totum et pars, et cognoscimus quod omne totum est majus sua parte, *considerando* hoc in pluribus." *In I Post. Analyt.,* lect. XXX (ed. Leonine vol. 1, p. 259, no. 5).

"Ad 2^m dicendum, quod iudicium non dependet tantum a receptione speciei, sed ex hoc quod ea de quibus iudicatur, examinantur ad aliquod principium cognitionis, sicut de conclusionibus iudicamus eas in principia resolvendo. . . . Sed quia primum principium nostrae cognitionis est sensus, oportet ad sensum quodammodo resolvere omnia de quibus iudicamus." *De Veritate* q. 12 a. 3.

23. "Dicendum quod in qualibet cognitione duo est considerare, scilicet principium et terminum. Principium quidem ad apprehensionem pertinet, terminus autem ad iudicium; ibi enim cognitio perficitur. Principium igitur cuiuslibet nostrae cognitionis est in sensu, quia ex apprehensione sensus oritur apprehensio phantasiae, quae est motus a sensu factus, ut dicit Philosophus, a qua iterum oritur apprehensio intellectiva in nobis, cum phantasmata sint intellectivae animae ut obiecta, ut patet in III de Anima." *In lib. Boethii de Trin.*, q. 6 a. 2 (ed. Paul Wyser, O.P., Louvain: E. Nauwelaerts, 1948, p. 63).

24. "Ad quintum dicendum quod phantasma est principium nostrae cognitionis, ut ex quo incipit intellectus operatio, non sicut transiens, sed sicut permanens, ut quoddam fundamentum intellectualis operationis, sicut principia demonstrationis oportet manere in omni processu scientiae, cum phantasmata comparentur ad intellectum ut obiecta, in quibus inspicit omne quid inspicit vel secundum perfectam repraesentationem vel per negationem. Et ideo quando phantasmatum cognitio impeditur, oportet totaliter impediri cognitionem intellectus etiam in divinis. Patet

enim quod non possumus intelligere Deum
esse causam corporum sive supra omnia corpora sive absque corporeitate, nisi imagine-
mur corpora, non tamen iudicium divinorum
secundum imaginationem formatur. Et ideo
quamvis imaginatio in qualibet divinorum
consideratione sit necessaria secundum statum viae, nunquam tamen ad eam deduci
oportet in divinis." *Ibid.*, ad 5 (p. 65).

25.   "Unde, cum similitudo rei quae est in in-
tellectu nostro, accipiatur ut separata a ma-
teria, et ab omnibus materialibus conditioni-
bus, quae sunt individuationis principia;
relinquitur quod intellectus noster, per se
loquendo, singularia non cognoscat, sed universalia tantum." *De Veritate* q. 2 a. 6.

26.   It is clear in St. Thomas that when *intellectus* is correlated with conceptual knowledge,
an understanding of the individual is excluded. Yet, in order to form the judgment
"Socrates is a man," intellectual knowledge
of the individual is necessary." (*Summa
Theol.* I q. 86 a. 1) Moreover, the same power
must be aware of both the "universal" applied
and the individual to which it is applied.
". . . Ita etiam non possemus cognoscere com-
parationem universalis ad particulare, nisi

esset una potentia quae cognosceret utrumque. Intellectus igitur utrumque cognoscit,
sed alio et alio modo." *In III De Anima*
lect. VIII (ed. Pirotta, no. 712).

St. Thomas describes the mode in which
intellectual knowledge attains the individual
by various expressions, *Indirecte, per quamdam reflexionem, per quamdam continuationem.* In any case the actual sense presentation
of the individual is required. 'Et ideo singularia non cognoscuntur in sua absentia nisi
per universalia," *In VII Metaph.*, lect. X
(Cathala no. 1496); ". . . illa, quorum est
definitio cognoscuntur per suam definitionem;
sed singularia non cognoscuntur nisi dum
sunt sub sensu vel imaginatione," *ibid.*, (no.
1495.)

The sense powers are said to assist the intellect in knowing the singular ("adminiculo
inferiorum virium," *In lib. Boethii de Trin.*,
q. 5 a. 2 ad 4). The term *"indirecte"* is reduced to the idea of union; "in quantum
[intellectus] coniungitur phantasiae, quae
repraesentat sibi phantasma: et sic indirecte
cognoscit [singularia in materia]," *Quodlibet.*,
q. 12 a. 11.

The *"reflexio"* is explained as a *continuatio*.
"Inquantum ergo intellectus noster per simili-

tudinem quam accepit a phantasmate, re-
flectitur in ipsum phantasma a quo speciem
abstrahit, quod est similitudo particularis,
habet quandam cognitionem de singulari secundum continuationem quamdam intellectus
ad imaginationem." *De Veritate* q. 2 a. 6.

We therefore have a situation in which the
intellectual knowledge of the individual involves the presence of a phantasm, of which
the intellect is aware and in which it finds
the material singular. Whether the context
concerns the application of a universal to the
particular, the operation of ethical knowledge
in particular cases or the experiential knowledge of an individual, the description is ba-
sically the same. This description outlines an
operational unity of intellect and sense in
which intellect uses the sense powers. The
key word, *continuatio,* was already a technical term in Arabian philosophy for just
such an operational unity of diverse powers.
A judgment concerning a material individual
(e.g. "Socrates is a man.") is possible only
through an intellectual awareness of and an
operational unity with the sense powers in
which the individual is presented. Both the
texts of Saint Thomas and the experiential re-
flexion used in our text lead to the same con-

clusion and reach agreement in the same description of the facts. For a significant collection of pertinent texts see G. Kennard, S.J., *The Intellect Composing and Dividing According to St. Thomas Aquinas* (unpublished thesis, Saint Louis University, 1949), chapter III, "The Necessity of Composition for Knowledge of the Temporal and the Particular," pp. 58-90; G. P. Klubertanz, S.J. *The Vis Cogitativa According to St. Thomas Aquinas: Sources and Doctrine* (unpublished thesis, University of Toronto, 1947), pp. 393-400, 428-35, 441-46; *idem,* "The Unity of Human Activity," *The Modern Schoolman* XXVII, (1950), pp. 75-103.

27. Cf. *De Veritate* q. 2 a. 7.

28. Cf. R. J. Henle, S.J. "Existentialism and the Judgment," *Proceedings of the American Catholic Philosophical Association,* Vol. XXI 1946), pp. 40-52.

29. Une métaphysique de l'être en tant qu'être "consignifie" l'existence, elle ne la "signifie" pas, à moins précisément qu'elle n'use de la deuxième opération de l'entendement et mette en oeuvre toutes les ressources du jugement. Le sentiment, si juste en soi, que le concept

universal d'être et le contraire d'une notion vide, trouvera là de quoi se justifier. Sa richesse est d'abord faite de tous les jugements d'existence qu'elle résume et qu'elle connote, mais plus encore de sa référence permanente à la réalité infiniment riche de l'acte pur d'exister. C'est pourquoi la métaphysique de saint Thomas poursuit, à travers l'essence de l'être en tant qu'être, cet existant suprême qu'est Dieu. Étienne Gilson, *Le Thomisme*, p. 67.

30. Lonergan, *loc. cit.*

The Aquinas Lectures

Published by the Marquette University Press,
Milwaukee 3, Wisconsin

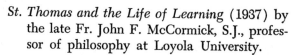

St. Thomas and the Life of Learning (1937) by the late Fr. John F. McCormick, S.J., professor of philosophy at Loyola University.

St. Thomas and the Gentiles (1938) by Mortimer J. Adler, Ph.D., associate professor of the philosophy of law, University of Chicago.

St. Thomas and the Greeks (1939) by Anton C. Pegis, Ph.D., president of the Pontifical Institute of Mediaeval Studies, Toronto.

The Nature and Functions of Authority (1940) by Yves Simon, Ph.D., professor of philosophy of social thought, University of Chicago.

St. Thomas and Analogy (1941) by Fr. Gerald B. Phelan, Ph.D., director of the Mediaeval Institute, University of Notre Dame.

St. Thomas and the Problem of Evil (1942) by Jacques Maritain, Ph.D., professor of philosophy, Princeton University.

Humanism and Theology (1943) by Werner Jaeger, Ph.D., Litt.D., "university" professor, Harvard University.

The Nature and Origins of Scientism (1944) by Fr. John Wellmuth, S.J., Chairman of the Department of Philosophy, Xavier University.

Cicero in the Courtroom of St. Thomas Aquinas (1945) by the late E. K. Rand, Ph.D., Litt.D., LL.D., Pope Professor of Latin, *emeritus*, Harvard University.

St. Thomas and Epistemology (1946) by Fr. Louis-Marie Régis, O.P., Th.L., Ph.D., director of the Albert the Great Institute of Mediaeval Studies, University of Montreal.

St. Thomas and the Greek Moralists (1947, Spring) by Vernon J. Bourke, Ph.D., professor of philosophy, St. Louis University, St. Louis, Missouri.

History of Philosophy and Philosophical Education (1947, Fall) Étienne Gilson of the Académie française, director of studies and professor of the history of mediaeval philosophy, Pontifical Institute of Mediaeval Studies, Toronto.

The Natural Desire for God (1948) by Fr. William R. O'Connor, S.T.L., Ph.D., professor of dogmatic theology, St. Joseph's Seminary, Dunwoodie, N. Y.

St. Thomas and The World State (1949) by Robert M. Hutchins, Chancellor of The University of Chicago.

Method in Metaphysics (1950) by Fr. Robert J. Henle, S.J., Dean of the Graduate School, St. Louis University, St. Louis, Missouri.

First in Series (1937) $1.00; all others $2.00
Uniform format, cover and binding.